The Crisis of Social Reproduction

Silvia Federici and
Mariarosa Dalla Costa

in conversation with Louise Toupin
Translated by Käthe Roth

Between the Lines
Toronto

First published in French by les Éditions du remue-ménage as *La crise de la reproduction sociale*, © Louise Toupin et les Éditions du remue-ménage, 2020. English translation by Käthe Roth, reprinted with permission of the publishers from *Wages for Housework: A History of an International Feminist Movement, 1972–77* by Louise Toupin © University of British Columbia Press and Pluto Press, 2018. All rights reserved by the publishers.

This edition published in 2025 by
Between the Lines
401 Richmond Street West, Studio 281
Toronto, Ontario · M5V 3A8 · Canada
1-800-718-7201 · www.btlbooks.com

Library and Archives Canada Cataloguing in Publication
Title: The crisis of social reproduction / Silvia Federici and Mariarosa Dalla Costa, in conversation with Louise Toupin ; translated by Käthe Roth.
Other titles: Crise de la reproduction sociale. English Names: Federici, Silvia, interviewee | Dalla Costa, Mariarosa, interviewee. | Toupin, Louise, interviewer | Roth, Käthe, translator
Series: Provocations (Toronto, Ont.)
Description: Series statement: Provocations | Translation of: La crise de la reproduction sociale. | In English, translated from the French.
Identifiers: Canadiana (print) 20240496809 | Canadiana (ebook) 20240496817 | ISBN 9781771136655 (softcover) | ISBN 9781771136662 (EPUB)
Subjects: LCSH: Federici, Silvia—Interviews. | LCSH: Dalla Costa, Mariarosa—Interviews. | LCSH: Women—Economic aspects. | LCSH: Women—Social conditions. | LCSH: Feminists—Italy. | LCSH: Feminism. | LCSH: Sexual division of labor. | LCSH: Unpaid labor. | LCSH: Housekeeping. | LCGFT: Interviews.
Classification: LCC HQ1381 .F4313 2025 | DDC 305.4201—dc23

Cover and text design by DEEVE
Printed in Canada

We acknowledge for their financial support of our publishing activities: the Government of Canada; the Canada Council for the Arts; and the Government of Ontario through the Ontario Arts Council, the Ontario Book Publishers Tax Credit program, and Ontario Creates.

Contents

Mariarosa Dalla Costa, International Day of Struggle
for Wages for Housework, May 1, 1975, Mestre (Venice)
(Mariarosa Dalla Costa Archives)

Interview with Mariarosa Dalla Costa[1]

Mariarosa Dalla Costa was born in Treviso, Italy, in 1943. She studied at the University of Padua, received her doctorate in law in 1967, and was a professor at the Istituto di Scienze Politiche e Sociali. She is the author of the founding document of the Wages for Housework perspective, *"Donne e sovversione sociale"* ("Women and the Subversion of the Community"), published in 1972 with an essay by Selma James, *"Il posto della donna"* ("A Woman's Place"), as *Potere femminile e sovversione sociale*. The book was translated into several languages, including into English as *The Power of Women and the Subversion of the Community*.

Louise Toupin: *Potere femminile* had an international impact in the feminist world when it was published in 1972, first in Italian, then in English. In the years that followed, it was translated into several other languages, forcing feminists of all tendencies to situate themselves in relation to the analysis that it propounded. Before diving into the content of the book, we could first talk about the context of its production in Italy and the ideological and political "soil" in which its ideas matured. That is, it would be interesting to spend a little time describing the intellectual and political conjuncture within which this book-manifesto was written.

First, I would like to know what influence the Italian workerist current, also called the "autonomy current," may have had on your thought. Then, what was the influence of the Italian and foreign feminist essays on housework that had begun to appear in 1969–70? Let's start with the workerist, or autonomy, current, an intellectual and political trend of the Italian extra-parliamentary left.

Some authors, such as Yann Moulier Boutang—the translator of Mario Tronti—who introduced the Italian workerist current into France, names you as one of "those who made a significant contribution" to the Italian workerist current. Another, Harry Cleaver, spoke of Selma James and you as being feminist theoreticians of "autonomist Marxism."[2] What do you think of this assessment, and how do you interpret it? And do you agree that *The Power of Women and the Subversion of the Community* matured in this intellectual soil?

Mariarosa Dalla Costa: My political formation began with workerism. I would not say with "autonomy," which is a definition formulated years later, when I was already active within the feminist movement, in the Wages for Housework movement. From the beginning, and throughout its life, that movement represented a reality that was completely independent of those male networks, including the ones labelled "autonomy." But I can understand why our discourses were later designated, as Harry Cleaver and then Nick Witheford did, as being "autonomous Marxism."[3] Indeed, starting from a

Marxist matrix, we chose the point of view of autonomy of the class movement, of a class that we had redefined, and that included women's work of production and reproduction of labour power.

The origins of the discourse on class autonomy are found, however, in works by C.L.R. James and Raya Dunayevskaya, as well as in the group around the magazine *Socialisme ou barbarie* in France, whose most prominent representatives were Cornelius Castoriadis and Claude Lefort.[4]

In fact, the significance of our work—mine and that of my friends in the Wages for Housework groups—is recognized as having been the discovery of the other pole of capitalist accumulation, the other path that it takes: production and reproduction of labour power. In other words, we discovered the home beside the factory. We discovered that the class was formed not only of waged workers but also of nonwaged workers.

Today, taking this into account is fundamental to understanding the "capitalist command," which, from the world of production, is deployed in forms that are ever more "strangling" and lethal in the world of reproduction.[5] It is also fundamental to understanding the relationship between the formal and informal economy, the relationship between the monetary and nonmonetary economy, and the relationship between the first world and the third world (to use a conventional shorthand). Also, to understanding the struggles that, arising from the world of global reproduction, tend to break this command, and to affirm other criteria in the relationship with production, with nature, and with life.

So, to answer your question: yes, *The Power of Women and the Subversion of the Community* matured in this workerist intellectual "soil." But I remember that there was some resistance, quite strong, from workerist intellectuals to broadening the concept of the working class to include, as we maintained in the early 1970s, houseworkers. Workerist theoreticians insisted that what we called production—that is, production and reproduction of labour power—belonged, rather, to the sphere of circulation, as Marx described in *Das Kapital*. When, later, they spoke of the "social worker" *(operaio sociale)*, they were alluding, rather, to different figures of workers in the context of the decentralization of production. They had recognized in the new political composition of class in the early 1970s the struggles of students and their demands for a wage for schoolwork, the technicians' struggle, and so on. But these intellectuals of the extra-parliamentary left seriously undervalued housework. I think their idea on this subject consisted of saying that women's problems would be solved with more and better-organized daycare centres. They believed more in solutions in terms of services. They always under-estimated the real scope of reproduction work and the impact of the lack of money on women who were assigned to this work.

And I also believe that most theoreticians in this current, after reading *The Power of Women* and gaining a vague idea of the issue, never read the other documents that we in Wages for Housework groups produced afterward. And I think that, even today, they are still not aware of the existence of this intellectual output. The consequence is that they continue to ignore almost completely the question of reproductive work and the entire political debate about it advanced by feminists.

However, in recent years, as we have entered a new stage in our analysis, some of our most recent work—and the most important part of our past work—is now translated into English, Spanish, and Japanese, and it will soon be available in other languages. This enables us to continue to contribute, in the best way, we hope, to an international political debate that must address questions that are increasingly urgent and tragic.

LT: Let's talk now about the feminist readings that fed into *The Power of Women and the Subversion of Community*. For example, what notable essays from Western feminism on housework had begun to circulate in Italy at the beginning of the 1970s, and were you aware of them when you were writing *The Power of Women?* I'm thinking here, among others, of Margaret Benston's 1969 text, *The Political Economy of Women's Liberation;* Christine Delphy's text published in 1970 (under the pseudonym Christine Dupont), *L'ennemi principal;* and, in 1970–71, those by Betsy Warrior, *Housework: Slavery or Labour of Love*, and Pat Mainardi, *The Politics of Housework*. In short, which feminist works had an impact on you at the time?

MDC: I didn't know about any of the foreign feminist works you mention. There had been Italian works on "women's condition" in general and on abortion. I think that the time was ripe, in Italy and abroad, for the issue to burst out, mainly because we were in a period of great social rebellion and struggles of all sorts. At the time I was completely absorbed by political activism and concentrating on Italian analyzes linked to my political work. My feminist discourse was the result of the explosion of contradictions that I was experiencing in my political activity.

This activity began at four o'clock in the morning—I had to get up to distribute leaflets in front of large factories—and it continued in the evenings, and on Saturdays and Sundays. If I don't mention that this was my type of life, it would be difficult to understand why I didn't read, at the time, some of the books on the question of women that were beginning to be published. Also, I am Italian. My knowledge of English was very limited at the time; I later learned the language during my feminist activism by travelling through, among other places, North America. I knew French, but I didn't have particularly meaningful or frequent relations with France.

LT: Were you Marxist first and then feminist, or were you feminist first and then Marxist? Basically, I want to know whether Marxism made you into a feminist, or whether your life experience made you a feminist first who later discovered Marxism.

MDC: Fundamentally, I was pushed into activism and into discovering the "factory" by an ideal of justice. I wanted to understand where the evil in the world came from, the origin of the mechanism, in a sense the *omphalos,* of the social relations system.[6] And that is how I encountered the workerist version of Marxism.[7] In itself, Marxism was a great discovery that gave me, and continues to give me, essential tools for understanding the world.

Political activism was the other great experience of my life because it provides thought with the coordinates for action. But, within this activism, I experienced, as did many other women in extra-parliamentary groups in the early 1970s, the contradiction of not feeling that my condition as a woman was represented or understood— neither by activism nor by this Marxist thought. Yet, that was what I was seeking.

My encounter with Selma James was fundamental in this respect. But our paths soon diverged due to a different conception of political action. To answer your question: yes, I was first Marxist, and then feminist; I have to add that my search for a different path from that which the society of the time expected of a young woman had obviously started long before.

LT: *The Power of Women and the Subversion of Community* contains three essays: yours, "Women and the Subversion of Community," written in early 1971; an essay by Selma James, "A Woman's Place," written in 1953; and an essay called "Maternity and Abortion" by the Paduan group Lotta Femminista; the introduction is written by James. Your essay "Women and the Subversion of Community," which was in circulation starting in June 1971, is historically linked to Lotta Femminista, though it preceded the group's formation.[8] In a way, it led to its birth. Can you share the circumstances under which you wrote this essay?

MDC: I had written a preliminary version of this text, copies of which were handed out for discussion to a group of female friends who were interested in feminism. It was signed "*Movimento di Lotta femminile di Padova*" (it was really an improvised name) and dated June 1971. This small group of friends recognized themselves in the analysis offered in the document. And soon after, the group became Lotta Femminista.

Later, I expanded this document and decided to publish it under the title *Potere femminile e sovversione sociale*. I thought it would be good to publish it, to ensure that it would be widely distributed. And that proved to be true. But I didn't have the time or sufficient mental calmness to take up in greater detail the series of questions that I would have liked to analyze better and develop because I was already absorbed in a very intense activist life. And I must say that I still struggle with time, even today, and for reasons that are closely related to those of that period.

I dedicated my 1971 Christmas vacation to verifying *Potere femminile* with Selma and to finalizing the book, which was aimed fundamentally at the movement and has become a classic in feminist curricula in the United States. I remember that Pia, feeling sorry for us, came over on the last day of the year with some spumante and panettone.[9] And it was also on a December 31, this time in 1995, that I put the final touches on a book analyzing the consequences of neoliberalism and structural adjustment policies on the condition of peoples—and women in particular—in the new situation of economic globalization.[10]

LT: You said, in a speech at a colloquium in Montreal, that because of the particular Italian context in the early 1980s, feminism in Italy was certainly marked, more strongly than that in other countries, by the issue of work/refusal of work.[11] Was this because of the intellectual influence of the workerist current, which had made refusal of work one of its central themes of analysis?

MDC: The theme of refusal of work made it possible to act and to struggle from the perspective of a draconian reduction in the workday. This was the only approach that could open new prospects for women. It went counter to the perspective proposed by the institutional left, with its labour ideology, that told women that adding another job to the work they were already doing in the home was the only future path. We denounced this. To calculate women's work, one should have started with the work that they were already doing, housework, and, on that basis, one had to conceive of a major reduction in their workday. In parallel, their financial autonomy should start with economic recognition of their work in the home. It was the same thing for men if, as might happen, they were the ones who did this work, or part of it.

LT: When one reads *The Power of Women and the Subversion of Community*, it is surprising that the Wages for Housework strategy is not mentioned as such, except in passing, in a footnote.[12] Does this mean that the Wages for Housework strategy was clarified after the theory was published? And if so, when or on which occasion did it appear?

MDC: Yes. I think that our main wish was to open a new perspective of struggle on the condition of women. But the determination of a Wages for Housework demand required that we take a little more time. However, even though the demand for a wage appears in a later edition of *Potere femminile,* it was inscribed very quickly in our internal documents.

I think that some of the uncertainty with regard to this subject came because we were aware that, to a large extent, it would have been very difficult to obtain such a thing, which would truly have opened up an alternative to women's condition. The capitalist system was based on precisely the opposite—on opposition between waged workers and nonwaged workers, mainly women as reproducers of labour power. This was very different from asking for a raise on an existing wage. On the one hand, we may have appeared unrealistic, but on the other hand, we knew that, like other struggling sectors of society, we truly wanted to create a different world, a different system, in which the subordination of one subject—in this case, a gendered subject—to another would become impossible. The Wages for Housework demand constituted, in this respect, the most radical claim we could make—a true lever of power for women because it could claim to subvert not only their condition but the condition of unwaged workers in general, as well as the condition of waged workers.

In fact, the waged work/unwaged work division represented the fundamental division within the working class in the broad sense, the basis for all other stratifications. In this sense, our demand constituted the pivot for the most powerful recomposition of class. And it wasn't by accident that, in reaction to such a recomposition, which was the expression of an international cycle of struggle representing the reunification of different sectors of working society, capital launched a political and economic counteroffensive. On the global level, this counteroffensive is still increasingly implacable. However, more and more subjects, from both the unwaged and the waged world, are emerging on the political scene and are capable of making their voices heard, such as Indigenous peoples—in Chiapas, for example.

LT: For you, the primary significance of the emergence of the women's movement was expression of women's massive revolt against their assignment to the material and immaterial work of reproduction, but it was also the expression of a profound rupture in the social order, a rupture in the balance that you have called "society/factory dependence relationships" in Italy. What do you mean by that?

MDC: What was in play with the explosion of the feminist movement—and I mean by this everything that the feminist movement agreed on—was women's willingness to assert themselves as persons, as social individuals—to assert their own reproductive needs, as a function of themselves as women, and no longer only as a function of the satisfaction of others' needs. This had enormous implications for the area of sexuality, for how a woman organized her own life, for how she lived (alone? with other women? with a group of people? so, not necessarily with a man), for her procreative choices. In this last area, the women in Italy expressed the greatest possible refusal of work, also as a function of self-affirmation.

The meaning of the emergence of the women's movement was to be found in the rupture of a purely functional relationship between reproduction and production, the rejection of modifications to the organization of reproduction induced solely as a function of changes in the world of production (for example, the fact that women would have to have more or fewer children as a function of the needs of production). The significance of this emergence was found in the assertion of women as autonomous social subjects as opposed to being, within the family, a simple appendage to economic programs. I developed this theme in "Reproduction and Emigration" by analyzing the state's attitude toward demographic policies and emigration.[13]

On the political level, it was a rupture from the preceding period: the assertion of women's autonomy meant struggling not only to support other subjects' struggles—in this case, those who were exploited within the factory—but to struggle in their own field of work, especially housework, which meant a broadening of the front of contestation and therefore an even more powerful struggle.

LT: In *The Power of Women and the Subversion of the Community*, you write that in their struggle regarding conditions of reproduction and against men-women-children dependency, women did not ask simply the question of their own autonomy, but they opened also another possibility: that of strengthening the autonomy of others. Can you expand your thinking on this point?

MDC: I can add this to what I have already said: it was not by chance that almost all the leaflets of the early period of the feminist movement ended by mentioning women, children, and the elderly. Because women had suffered so much oppression and so much exploitation, they became, through actions by the feminist movement, the most sensitive interpreters of the cause of other oppressed subjects—and, above all, children and old people, who, in a situation of weakness, depended on their work and therefore constituted a strong point for their demands. Historically, women often identified themselves with other oppressed subjects, helped them, and stood by their side in their struggles.

In this regard it is significant to observe that as soon as the feminist question arose in Italy in the early 1970s, the institutional discourse on the family was also transformed to take into account the rights of children as persons, and those of the elderly, the disabled, and the ill. I don't mean that the social and material situation in Italy was vastly improved. Indeed, it would be very difficult to support such an idea. But the social and political debate that we provoked opened, also on the institutional level, a new space for consideration of different oppressed subjects, and it stimulated practical initiatives that had not existed before.

LT: Let's talk about the theoretical innovations of *Potere femminile*. We could mention the new comprehension of the role played by the family in capitalist society (a centre of production and not just of consumption), of the position of women and of the work that they do in the family (producer and reproducer of labour power), and of women's power (if they do productive work, by refusing this work they may subvert society). Women thus are reintroduced into history as subjects—and revolutionary subjects. Another thing that was new was the Wages for Housework demand as a lever of power, to begin the "negotiation on reproduction." Do you agree with this summary of the theoretical innovations of *Potere femminile*? And when you look back, what do you think was the most important thing you said?

MDC: You bring up key points. Before mentioning others, I want to remind you that *Potere femminile*, like the other documents that we produced, was inscribed in a Marxian horizon of analysis—that is, these documents express a discourse from a class point of view, broadened in our own way. This means that our privileged object/subject was women who *reproduced* individuals as *holders of labour power*—that is, women who lived materially within a proletarian condition.

But we also emphasized, in numerous documents and articles, the particular precariousness of many women's class affiliation. Indeed, as the feminist movement developed, the movement constituted an anchor point, a key element in the construction of a new identity for women. Many of them had then left marriages that had guaranteed them a certain social standing. From one day to the next, they found themselves facing the question of economic survival and obliged to perform precarious work, as it was quite difficult to imagine that the husbands they had just left would support them financially. The struggle of women of the working class (as we had redefined it), because it was aiming for a radical change in the world, was decisive in the opening of new perspectives and life possibilities for all women.

There is another point in *Potere femminile* that I consider fundamental, particularly today, in the context of the new global economy. I hope you don't mind if I quote a few passages on the subject. Here's one:

> Since Marx, it has been clear that capital rules and develops through the wage, that is, that the foundation of capitalist society was the wage laborer and his or her direct exploitation. What has been neither clear nor assumed by the organizations of the working class movement is that precisely through the wage has the exploitation of the nonwage laborer been organized. This exploitation has been even more effective because the lack of a wage hid it. That is, the wage commanded a larger amount of labor that appeared in factory bargaining. *Where women are concerned, their labor appears to be a personal service outside of capital.*

And here's another:

> The rule of capital through the wage compels every able-bodied person to function, under the law of division of labor, and to function in ways that are

if not immediately, then ultimately profitable to the expansion and extension of the rule of capital.[14]

And so, we can say that capital, in the family, through the husband's wage, commands the wife's work in the home. But this relationship can be read elsewhere, as much in the relationship between the monetary and the nonmonetary economy, between the new global economy and the subsistence economy, and in the new divisions of labour within production and reproduction. For example, through waged work that an emigrant worker finds in New York, capital also commands the agricultural work of the wife who, having remained in her village, continues to maintain that economic structure, which constitutes life insurance for the worker if he must or wants to return to the village.

It is important to keep all of this in mind in order to grasp, in the current global scenario, the cycles of struggle that tend to break this capitalist reign. This theme continues to be central in my work, such as, for example, "Capitalism and Reproduction," "*L'indigeno che è in noi, la terra cui apparteniamo,*" and "*Neo- liberismo, terra e questione alimentare,*" and in the books that I edited with my sister, Giovanna Franca, *Donne e politiche del debito* and *Donne, sviluppo e lavoro di riproduzione.*[15] This theme is also at the heart of Giovanna Franca's book *Un lavoro d'amore,* published in Italy in 1978: she analyzes, in particular, the function of physical violence by the man, who, as a waged worker, commands, controls, and maintains discipline over the woman's unwaged work.[16] This theme is also central to the writings of Silvia Federici.

LT: How do you interpret the enormous international impact on the feminist movement of *The Power of Women and the Subversion of the Community* in the 1970s, and how do you interpret the failure of the strategy that accompanied it?

MDC: In my view, the book had an enormous impact not only because the analysis hit the mark but also because it was felt that it came from a world that was spirited, activist, and gave direction for action. The book highlighted the idea of capital as social relations and class relations to be destroyed and not simply as something to improve or as a quantity of wealth to distribute more fairly. This was the difference between revolutionary feminism and reformist feminism.

Those years were part of a cycle of struggles that had developed at the international level starting in the second half of the 1960s, aimed at breaking the bases and balances of capitalism, in both East and West, in both North and South. And Italy, more specifically, saw during the 1970s a massive mobilization of workers, students, unemployed people, technicians, and people from other key sectors of the work world.

The feminist movement emerged from this framework of struggle. Activists from different countries, sympathetic with our perspective, or who had espoused this perspective, decided to translate and use *Potere femminile*, as well as the rich group of analyses and documentation materials produced by our groups, composed of our journals, newsletters, leaflets, mimeographed texts, and booklets published and designed for activist use.[17]

From this heritage were formed not only activist women but also several generations of women who occupied positions at different levels in institutions and universities. They had mastered the discourses but, unfortunately, often erased the origins, the sources, and the real scope of this discourse and raised obstacles of many kinds to the possibility of the existence and dissemination of later steps in the evolution of this type of analysis.

Why have we not succeeded? Well, for the same reasons for which the other sectors in struggle were defeated. Because against so powerful a cycle of struggles, which caused a very important recomposition of class power, above all between waged and unwaged work, the capitalist system responded by decentralizing production, changing the conditions of production, causing much unemployment, destabilizing work, lowering salaries, and making draconian reductions in public expenditures destined for social purposes. And this is increasingly true today [here, Dalla Costa is talking about the mid-1990s], making the possibilities for life, in general, very uncertain.

The systematic application around the world of structural adjustment policies, in the name of managing the international debt crisis, provoked underdevelopment of reproduction on a planetary level. In many countries, the 1980s were a decade of popular uprisings and struggles for bread. In Italy, they were years of political repression and "normalization." The history of the feminist Wages for Housework movement and the works of its theoreticians were practically erased from the feminist scene and from feminine culture in general and were ignored in university curricula. This was true not only for works written in the 1970s but also for works published in the early 1980s, which were fundamental to the later formulation of this discourse.[18]

In Italy, the response by the capitalist system was even harder in the 1990s, related to what was going on all over the world. As I analyzed it in two essays in those years ("*Capitalismo e riproduzione*" and "*Sviluppo e riproduzione*"[19]), in Italy we saw phenomena such as suicides due to lack of work or due to refusal to accept the only job offered because the employer was a criminal organization, cases of people trying to sell their organs to make money, cases of mothers who abandoned their child immediately after birth, the fact that a large part of the population was in debt to moneylenders, and so on.

The Gulf War was a kind of shock for Italian society. People in Italy had to reconsider the idea of sending their sons to die in the war. So, they began again to reflect on the world at a social level, the effects of this economic system, and what could be done. A new political debate arose, on the basis of discussion about the possibility of constructing other production, consumption, and life relations, other relations with nature and with all living beings. These last themes, more particularly, although expressed by a minority in the movement's debate, went counter to an institutional discourse that, submitted to the constantly more constraining structural adjustment directives imposed by the International Monetary Fund, completely shut off the social question and the question of relations with nature, starting with relations with the land and with food.

The Chiapas rebellion and the movement that represented it—within which women played a fundamental role—as well as a number of struggles and movements around the world that aimed for a different kind of development, different above all because they were not capitalist, constituted one indication, one possible alliance. At the same time it was a huge social and political laboratory for experimenting with inventions and new practices of production, consumption, and living, for the unwaged and the waged, men and women, throughout the world.

LT: How would you describe the stages in the evolution of your thought? How was the Wages for Housework perspective transformed through changes in the Italian and international conjunctures, and, finally, how would you update the Wages for Housework demand today?

MDC: The first thing to say about the evolution of my thought is that it is not integrated into an absolutely linear life path—that is, without interruptions or obstacles. Not only did I travel the world with a woman's body—and that means biological deadlines and conditioning—but work, responsibilities, and difficulties typical of the gender to which I belong formed obstacles, at different times of my life, to the possibility of giving written expression to thoughts and problems that I was wondering about. These obstacles, however, constituted at the same time a terrain of inspiration and analysis.

The very fact of having a privileged intellectual and activist life involved fairly heavy costs and renunciations of all sorts for me. But everything I did was certainly not done without paying the costs.

In the late 1970s and during the 1980s, I was absorbed with the task of confronting the consequences of political repression: helping people, including myself, to safeguard our heritage—that is, to keep everything that we produced during our activism of the 1970s from simply being destroyed; confronting an internal political debate that saw the painful necessity of dissolving our network and closing our women's centres.[20]

In the late 1970s, an era was ending. Activism based on a maximum of activities, on the one hand, and the lack of money that each of us could put into it, on the other hand, had brought us to a breaking point. Unlike what exists now for different women's initiatives, there was no articulation of funding on the national and international levels.

Incidentally, I wonder what limits, risks, and ambiguities today's initiatives may encounter because of this. It seems that the same logic at work in other major questions, such as the aggravated hardship of peoples of the world, on the one hand, and the burgeoning of initiatives funded for and around this hardship, on the other hand, is also at work in the women's question. Indeed, it is impossible to ignore the massive deterioration in women's condition in the world. The risk is to see the numbers of professionals in women's hardship growing ever larger and a female bureaucracy controlling the rebellion and the attempts to construct radical struggles against all of this—that is, against this type of development, in its new neoliberal expressions: structural adjustment policies, wars, continual expropriation of peoples' means of production, all oriented toward a single goal: everything must become a commodity, especially a commodity for export.

Let's return to our period in the late 1970s. Our organization found itself needing to transition to a new stage, as it was becoming obvious that the state would not grant us wages for housework. However, we had won at other levels: affirmation of a female identity no longer defined solely as a function of marriage, family, and children; affirmation of a female sexuality no longer defined solely as a function of procreation; affirmation of women's rights with regard to healthcare structures, abortion, childbirth, and, more generally, the types of treatments offered in obstetrics and gynecology departments (although much remains to be done in this area in several hospitals); we had achieved changes in the family code, and in many other things.

As for the question of wages for housework and economic conditions in general, we had not only a negative response, but again, as was the case for the other movements, a repressive response. Confronting all of this absorbed much of my time and activity.

With regard to my intellectual production during the 1980s, most importantly I finished the book on the relationship between women and the state during the New Deal—that is, during the phase of construction of the welfare state in the United States.[21] This book was intended to be a study of the birth of the blueprint of the women/welfare state/mode of production relationship, which was to form the dominant model in Western countries up to the 1970s. At the same time, in this study, the women's struggles that accompanied this model, alongside those of workers and unemployed people, were read as expression of the desire for autonomy.

In the United States, the 1930s were the testing ground for the modern family in a time of crisis: the woman houseworker was to administer the husband's salary (when he had one), but she also had to be available for work outside, above board or under the table, and at the same time she had to support the family in a context of high male unemployment, an insecure job market, and a new social security system.

If the 1930s marked the birth of the welfare state in the United States, the 1980s marked the beginning of its dismantlement. Whereas during the 1930s the idea was to adapt reproduction of labour power to production of goods within the framework of creating an overall productive and social plan, in the 1980s reproduction was left to the "free initiative" of individuals, and production of goods was gradually moved abroad in an international context of escalating war.

Despite the context having changed since the 1930s, the constraints on women continued to be the same during the 1980s, just as they are today, under conditions that are simply more difficult. How have women been able to continue, in this context, to build their autonomy? I have written articles on the subject in which I concentrated on public expenditures or employment policies in Italy.[22] In other articles, I have continued to reflect on the feminist movement of the 1970s, the crucial questions that it posed, and the struggles that it led.[23] This type of reflection is sometimes present in other articles that I have mentioned, such as the articles on public expenditures or employment. All of these works were conceived under very difficult conditions. I was always concerned with recording at least a few reflections in the face of a firestorm of events that was going to bury our world—the feminism of great struggles—in the dust of repression and normalization.

Another important theme that runs through many of my writings is demystification of the discourse by which strategies would be offered to women to reconcile work in the family and work outside the home. Female academics who exalted the "double presence" of women during the 1990s did not explain how many of them had resolved the housework problem.[24]

On this subject, I think that there were not, and still are not, many possible family strategies. There are only two. And it is particularly true in a country such as Italy, characterized by a very deficient, very expensive services system. Either women go to work outside and give up having children, thus avoiding the most important and the most problematic part of housework—this way, they may be able to combine housework and work outside—or women who have children will work outside by receiving support in the form of free help (in fact, work) from other women, generally relatives, or by paying other women to do part of the housework. But, in this case, the money given to these women must not cancel out what they themselves earn. Because of this, the amount of money received by the woman who comes into the home when the first one leaves is very small.

Thus, the problem is not resolved and results in an extra stratification among women. And, as I wrote in essays in the early 1980s—in which I analyzed the restructuring of productive and reproductive work that took place in Italy through the new immigration flows—immigrant women, mainly Filipinas, gradually assumed a large part of the housework, particularly care of children, the elderly, the disabled, and the ill.[25]

LT: You have written that two fundamental encounters forged your intellectual development starting in the 1990s: that with Indigenous movements (the trigger of which was reading *I, Rigoberta Menchú*) and that with ecofeminists (particularly Vandana Shiva).[26] Would you say that these encounters with women from the southern hemisphere caused a shift in your intellectual and activist journey?

MDC: On the whole, there was a shift. By analyzing the condition of women and men in terms of wages and time, I discovered a framework that was simply going to deteriorate. But, up to a certain point, I also felt that struggles in the field of work time and wages were too limited because they left to capital the initiative of defining the type of world and the type of life on earth.

Not only had we not won on the question of wages, but this struggle did not take account of the policies of production of death and misery that gradually castrated the reproductive powers of nature, of the land, and of the bodies of human beings in general. So, on the one hand, there was our struggle to obtain money and time for ourselves, which was a field we had to fight in, but, on the other hand, we also had to fight in a different field to not leave to the adversary all of the initiative for defining "which world" and "which life."

Above all, we had to consider the question of the land, which was constantly being increasingly privatized, expropriated, poisoned. This question involved, first, thinking about what, from our point of view, would be an acceptable agricultural solution for the inhabitants of the globe—a solution that would avoid having only poison available to buy to feed ourselves and that would leave room for access to "fresh and healthy food," to quote the slogan of a movement that was spreading particularly in the 1990s in both the southern and northern hemispheres.[27]

This issue continued to explode, in Italy and in the rest of the world, as could be observed during demonstrations by farmers who occupied the roads with their animals and agricultural products in 1997, 1998, and 1999. It played a central role in my works, within a critique of neoliberal structural adjustment policies—that is, of this type of development.[28] It even plays a central role in the attention that I pay to movements and initiatives by Indigenous peoples, and in the southern hemisphere in general, to construct other types of economies and lives. This is evidenced in my attention to the struggle in Chiapas since it began.

I would like to say in this regard that there was a significant difference between Marcos (leader of the

Zapatista movement in Chiapas) and other political leaders that I greatly appreciated: he was particularly sensitive to the difficulties experienced by women, members of the Revolutionary Army, living under extremely precarious conditions in the mountains, difficulties with their bodies and, every month, having their menstrual periods. He recognized this, he talked about it, and he took account of these biological differences in the struggle.[29]

LT: You have spoken of the "lethal process" that increasingly characterizes capitalist development today. What do you mean by this term?

MDC: It is well known that the capitalist economy is founded and continues to develop on the production of misery and death and on the uprooting and transferring of entire strata of populations. These processes function to weaken organization and resistance networks that populations have formed—that is, they weaken the reproductive powers of populations.

These processes were very obvious even early in the history of capital, during the period called primitive accumulation.[30] Today, populations continue to be uprooted and displaced because of major development projects by the World Bank (hydroelectric projects, in particular), or they occur as an effect of adjustment policies and variations in agricultural prices, forcing enormous contingents of people to emigrate.

On another level, there is also, in my opinion, a different type of policy for uprooting individuals, which is related to new reproductive technologies that tend to treat individuals more and more as laboratory products than as children of a biological mother and father in the context of their social relations. It is also a way of depriving individuals of the context of these relations, of their history, of their memory, which is also transmitted down the generations. It is to deprive individuals of their roots and their past. This is a policy of weakening individuals by weakening the construction of their identity, because the very ground on which it was first constructed has disintegrated.

Similarly, the policies of production of death and creation of misery are propagated in new configurations. Death and misery are increasingly conveyed through the continual production of morbidity and disabilities of all sorts, flowing from a neoliberalization of science that, through repeated experimentations that no one has authorized and no one has been able to stop up to now, brings new risks of disease, known or unknown, to weigh on people's bodies.

The continual wars taking place also offer the most convenient opportunity to experiment with all of this on a large number of living-dying test subjects. What is at play is the interruption of human bodies' reproductive powers, as those of the bodies of other living beings— plants and animals—have already been interrupted, in such a way as to render human bodies evermore dependent on medical science or, in other words, on the laboratory-market. This is an overall plan for castration of the reproductive powers of nature, the bodies of all living beings.

I think that it is not by accident that, while I was

considering, theoretically and practically, the struggles of populations against what I call the castration of the soil, which has occurred during the different stages from the green revolution to the arrival of new technologies, bio-technologies, and genetic manipulations of living beings, I met on my way, as have many women, the medical proposition of hysterectomy.

LT: In your intellectual path, you took on this issue of hysterectomy. What took you there?

MDC: The surgery was proposed to me, as it was to many other women, for no reason. I had the capacity and the possibility to verify the situation, and I refused it. But is this the case for many women? The confrontations that I had in this regard with other women and other doctors in order to verify the basis (or lack of basis) for the proposal opened my eyes to the practice: beyond the cases where it may prove necessary, it has become, in this century, a practice of mass castration of women in many advanced countries, and for reasons that certainly are not related to the well-being of women.

In fact, I discovered a shockingly frequent use of this surgery by doctors. I discovered all the negative consequences that are not usually mentioned when women are subjected to the operation, even though, in many cases, there are other, nonmutilating solutions that are not brought to their attention or offered as possible alternatives.

I saw the same aggressive, castrating policy that did harm to the reproductive powers of nature-land do harm here to the reproductive powers of the nature-body of women, each of whose organs is intimately linked to the entirety of the body. Only mechanistic, reductionist thinking would manage to isolate these powers, and isolate uterus and ovaries, setting aside the very complexity of the functions of these organs in relation to the body as a whole, and consider them simply superfluous after a certain age.

In my view, this hysterectomy problem arose as the third station, the third stage of the struggle, after those we had had to organize around childbirth and abortion, that punctuated the life path of women's bodies.

I decided to put forth the question and open the debate in Italy. After working alone for a few months, I prepared my first long presentation, which I would make as an invited speaker to a national conference of gynecologists in Palermo, on December 7, 1997.[31] It was a very important event, in terms of a confrontation between the discourse of a feminist woman and the discourses of doctors. I then organized a colloquium with gynecologists, but also with magistrates, on this same theme in Padua in 1998; a large number of women were in attendance.

I had invited magistrates, among other reasons, because I had come to the conclusion—and this was the thesis I presented in Padua, as I had in Palermo—that unjustified hysterectomies constituted an attack on the psychophysical integrity of the individual, a crime of very serious personal injury and, at the same time, a terrible form of violence perpetrated by medical science on women's bodies.[32] Then, I also organized a very big conference on the question in Venice with the participation of doctors, human rights specialists, jurists, and numerous women. After that, I was invited to a number of medical congresses in Rome and Milan. But this mobilization mainly offered an opportunity to come into contact with French female gynecologists and to participate in their great struggle to maintain the specialty of medical gynecology alongside that of surgical gynecology, instead of having only the latter, as the new policies would have had it. Women's bodies have always had difficulty traversing this world designed for men.

I remember a definition that we gave for "woman" during the 1970s. It went something like this: "A woman is a subject who, whatever she is doing, must interrupt herself if there is an emergency in the family." Once again, I found myself with the obligation of interrupting what I was doing: my research on the question of land. It was, however, not family in this case, but my own body, the body of a woman who had to fight another obstacle to be able to continue her life's journey.

LT: What have been your intellectual and activist concerns since 2000?

MDC: I have devoted these years to analyzing the discourses and struggles of the peasants' and fishers' movements under globalization. For the first few years, I concentrated on peasants' movements. I observed, in effect, that despite the bitter, long struggles conducted by different subjects, it is truly difficult to be able to imagine how an alternative to this type of development, another plan for social organization and production, could be constructed. The dominant model was reproduced continuously through expropriation of land, just as it had been in early capitalism, but in new forms—by appropriating and overturning nature's reproductive powers. This model of development is perpetuated through different types of expropriation, through which masses of people are expelled. The workers' condition is rebuilt on the planetary level and restratified on terms that approach slavery.

The overturning of mechanisms for spontaneous reproduction of life (by patents on seeds, for example), international debt, and structural adjustment programs are all components of a single strategy through which capital tends to create a food dictatorship involving maximum dependence by populations and in which these populations find themselves in conditions of absolute blackmail. We have to start from this question: How can this dictatorship be broken? Otherwise, it would be as if all the activism, all the struggles in the world, would be reduced to building a house without a foundation.

The peasants' movement addressed the problem of how to build this foundation. The desire to regraft the relationship between human life and the land, the negation of which constitutes the very soul of capitalist development, means reversing the conditions of this development and laying the basis for building a different kind of development—different first and foremost because it would not involve an increase in hunger and death as a fundamental premise.

The peasants' movement laid the groundwork for opposing the hunger strategy: food was a common good;

it involved the right of populations to have access to food sources—above all land, water, and biodiversity—and the fundamental freedom to choose what to eat and how to produce it; a democracy had to begin by being a food democracy; food sovereignty is a true source of food security. Many other themes were central to this movement: responsible agriculture is responsible to other peasants, to consumers, and to the land itself; the idea that food security could derive from the availability of hard currency that makes it possible to buy foodstuffs from multinationals must be rejected. From my point of view, it was important not to deal with these themes as if they concerned only the southern hemisphere. Different movements around the world, including in Italy, were moving in the same direction, and I analyzed what they had and didn't have in common, but on the whole they were converging.[33] In the meantime, a broad consumers' movement in the cities joined the peasants' movement so that this movement, in Italy for example, became more and more a rural-urban movement.[34]

At a certain stage of my research in this field, I presumed that if such social forces were at work with regard to the question of the land, similar forces must be at work on the question of the ocean, the rivers, the lakes, and the water that flows in the veins of the earth. And I found the fishers' movement, whose activities had begun in Kerala, India, in the 1970s, and had quickly gone global.

This encounter with the sea, with the ocean, like my encounter with the land, arose because this research corresponded to a need that I felt deep within me, the need to tie my life to that of nature.[35] It was above all a poetic encounter. It is not by chance that in the book that Monica Chilese and I wrote about the ocean, I devoted several verses to the sea.[36]

The fishers' movement against the gigantic fishery conducted on ships outfitted with high-technology equipment posed the question of responsible fishing, practised with a sense of limits and responsibilities with regard to other fishers, coastal populations, and the sea. The fishers' movement posed the central question of the need to safeguard the organic connection between the trade of fisher and maintenance of the ecosystem. It expressed the need to develop an eco-friendly, rather than a destructive, relationship with the ecosystem and asserted that the real possibility for abundance resided in defence of the spontaneous reproduction of sources and cycles of life.[37]

LT: What is the link between this research on the questions of land and sea and your previous research on the situation of women and their movement?

MDC: The question of the land and the sea, the question of food policies, on the one hand, and that of the movements for an alternative food system, on the other hand, enabled me to approach the question of reproduction and relaunch it at a higher level. The struggles around money and time were not enough to enable us to imagine a different future that did not immediately presume the growth of hunger in the world. The dominant food system produced not only hunger, however, but also disease.

Food scandals emerged in recent years. Traditionally a source of joy, food gradually became a source of suspicion and fear. The task of providing food, one of the primordial tasks of women's reproductive work, was now, as if randomly, facing many new problems: not only was food becoming rare, in both the southern and northern hemispheres, but it was also becoming unhealthy. As a consequence, in a number of regions, women were leading movements to preserve the land and food.

Furthermore, women who had traditionally taken care of the bodies of others had learned, with the women's movement of the 1970s, to take care of their own bodies. With determination, they raised questions about their autonomy and the satisfaction of their own desires, instead of living simply as a function of the satisfaction of others' needs.

Women's struggle to reappropriate their bodies did not concern just reappropriation of the knowledge and power to decide on procreation and their sexuality. They also refused to be machines for reproducing labour power and intended to reappropriate their own bodies as creative and desiring bodies. In opposition to a life completely devoted to work, they wanted to find time for themselves. In opposition to a femininity consisting solely of availability to satisfy others' needs, they intended to regain the right to emotions.

But today, the right to emotions and sensations is at the heart of the peasant agriculture movement because peasants refuse the ugliness that destruction of landscapes brings in its wake; they reject the sensory deprivation that the countryside generates, the abolition and standardization of flavours, and the destruction of knowledge. The right to creativity and beauty is very present in this movement, as is the right to food security. After this long industrial and urban winter, the bodies of women, and the bodies of others along with them, will be able to blossom again only with the blossoming of the land-body.[38]

At a certain point in my research, I decided to sort through all the materials I had, the materials for activist use and the more theoretical materials that I had either gathered or produced during my lifetime, in order to deposit them as an archive to be available to future generations. Some materials go back to the 1970s, but others are more concerned with the present day. There are materials on paper, such as leaflets, brochures, songs, and plays, and there are old records, cassettes, and films that I transferred onto CD or DVD.

I spent a few years collecting and ordering all of it, and in September 2011, I gave the entire collection to the municipal library in Padua, having been assured that it would do archival work and make it accessible to the public as soon as possible, as I had already put it in good order. This archive, with its millions of pieces, is now accessible for consultation by young (and old) generations.[39]

Mariarosa Dalla Costa (Photo: Dario De Bortoli)

Silvia Federici and Ruth Hall at
the London Conference of the
International Feminist Collective,
July 24–26, 1975
(Silvia Federici Archives)

Interview with Silvia Federici[1]

Silvia Federici was born in Parma, Italy, in 1942. She has lived in the United States since 1967, and in 1980 she earned a PhD in philosophy from the State University of New York at Buffalo. She is a professor emeritus of social sciences at Hofstra University in Hempstead, New York, and the author of key works substantiating the Wages for Housework perspective, including her seminal work *Wages against Housework* (Bristol: Falling Wall Press, 1975).

Louise Toupin: After all these years, and to give today's feminists an understanding of what the Wages for Housework project meant, could you share some lessons that can be drawn from the life of the International Feminist Collective (IFC)?

Silvia Federici: The IFC served to launch the International Wages for Housework campaign. It was therefore a very strong political experiment that deeply affected the lives of the women who took part in it.

To understand the meaning of our participation in this political project, one has to be aware of the general climate of the time. It was a revolutionary period for many women. We were coming from the movement—the student movement, the antiwar movement, the civil rights and anticolonial movements. We were certain that we were part of a process of historic transformation. And, in addition, we were active in the feminist movement, which was promising to completely change our lives. The experiences of those years were unique experiences that are possible only during specific historical periods, times when the "bottom rises up" and all of society seems to be in complete upheaval.

As for the experience in the Wages for Housework campaign, its power resided in the fact that it gave us great comprehension of society and the mechanisms of exploitation, and at the same time it touched the most personal aspects of our lives while enabling us to connect to all other women with a new sense of solidarity. It was a perspective that allowed us to encompass and also to step beyond the entire spectrum of women's experiences. I must add to this the feeling of power that came to us from having lived a collective life, a life in which women came first; for all of us, that was our primary interest.

And then there was the joy of seeing our skills and talents develop. We began to learn how to write texts and speak in public, write songs, make posters, analyze the newspapers day after day, and find our life interesting.

The lesson to be drawn? Learn to make a "sustainable revolution." The feminist movement upset the world, but it did not create the structures necessary to support its revolution (I'm talking about the strategic question of reproduction, which was left behind). The new political generations of women, if they want to complete our work, would do well not to forget that.

LT: But more precisely, what are the specific lessons to be drawn from the experience of the IFC?

SF: The campaign showed the importance of having an international network for an exchange of knowledge, materials, and struggle experiences, giving us the capacity to cooperate on many levels, to communicate about our struggle with a coherent vision, and, periodically, to evaluate the effectiveness of our work.

At the same time, this experience showed us the limits of any organization that exists in the absence of a mass movement. One of the limits of the International Wages for Housework campaign was the tendency to interpret the leadership role in a way that was too rigid, centralized, and hierarchical. This would not have been possible if it had been a mass movement, in which people make decisions autonomously, without waiting for permission from leadership.

LT: How did the Wages for Housework perspective influence your activism and your intellectual trajectory after 1977, after the IFC came to an end?

SF: The wage perspective made me understand that capitalism is a production system that depends structurally on noncontractual and unpaid work, in all its forms, and a system that devalues the reproduction of labour power. So, capitalism must continually create classes of workers with no rights who have the task of reproducing labour power at low cost. This is why capitalism, historically, was always essentially a structurally sexist and racist system. Sexism and racism are not moral problems. They are ideological and practical systems that serve to justify and conceal unwaged work regimes. Unpaid work is justified by the use of psychological and mental characteristics.

That is why I say that capitalism cannot be reformed. The Wages for Housework perspective showed me that there is an urgent need to build, from our daily struggles, an alternative to the capitalist system. My interest in the question of the commons springs from that.

The wage perspective also helped me understand the function of underdevelopment and the political significance, starting in the late 1970s, of the restructuring of the world economy as a process of "primitive accumulation"—that is, as an attack on the most fundamental means of our reproduction and the value of labour power.[2] This comprehension was reinforced by my stay in Nigeria in the mid-1980s, during which I saw the effects of globalization—in the form of the debt crisis and structural adjustment policies—on the population's living conditions.

My stay in Nigeria opened a new political horizon for me because, for the first time, I was in a country in which the majority of the population was still living off the land, and the land was still owned by the community. I understood then that the Wages for Housework struggle was only one aspect of the struggle for valourization of the work of reproduction and the construction of an alternative to capitalism.

LT: Could you explain the link between the question of land and Wages for Housework?

SF: The link is that in many countries, women's struggle around reproduction begins with reappropriation of the land, the land being the first and most fundamental means of reproduction in that when we talk about "the land," we are also talking about water, forests, agriculture, and food production.

At first, I thought that women's struggles for land were the equivalent, the counterpart, of Wages for Housework in industrialized countries. However, I observe that, even in Europe and North America, the struggle concerning the land has been reopened. In New York, new waves of immigrants from the Caribbean and Latin America (the new diaspora induced by globalization) provoked the development of a network of urban food-producing gardens, which brought together people from different countries to build a community and thus created elements of independence from the market. Even more important, the ecology, antiglobalization, and, especially, eco-feminist movements taught us that land, and not money, is the fundamental means of reproduction. If we don't have access to the land, we have nothing. We are very vulnerable to monetary manipulations and also to manipulations of food production. Of course, there is no question of turning ourselves into farm owners jealously guarding "their" land, but the question of land is fundamental to winning autonomy and also for regeneration of the planet.

In Nigeria, I learned from African women's struggles, first against colonization and then against "development," that loss of land has meant an enormous loss of power, especially for women. Access to land and the production of harvests—harvests that women could once use for their own reproduction and that of their children or to sell in the marketplace—were the basis of women's social power. Even today, this dispossession strengthens women's dependence on men.

Each new phase of "development," each new economic recovery program, inevitably involves privatization of the land, and women are the first victims.

LT: Talk about your activism after 1977, after your participation in the New York Wages for Housework Committee.

SF: After my involvement in the Wages for Housework campaign ended, I participated in different movements. First I formed, with other women, a group that produced the journal *Tap Dance,* in which we analyzed the economic and social dimensions of the neoliberal project, especially Reaganism. In *Tap Dance,* we also protested against the plan to recruit women into the army, which was supported by liberal feminist organizations.

In the 1990s, I began to participate in the Midnight Notes Collective and contributed to producing several issues of its magazine (of the same name, *Midnight Notes*).[3] Being in the collective helped me to interpret the "debt crisis" in Nigeria and to understand that this "crisis" was the instrument of a new process of enclosure and primitive accumulation.

In Nigeria, I worked with the feminist organization WIN (Women in Nigeria), and I helped write one of the documents that WIN presented at the 1985 Nairobi Conference.[4]

I also continued my historical and political research on the development of capitalism that I had begun in the 1970s. Between 1977 and 1983, I had cowritten a book with an Italian feminist, Leopoldina Fortunati, *The Great Caliban: Story of the Rebel Body in the First Phase of Capitalism* (published in Italian in 1984), in which we discuss the reorganization of reproduction during the period of transition from feudalism to capitalism.[5] During this project, I found what would become one of my main research subjects: the witch hunt, the persecution that inaugurated the history of women in capitalist society in the fifteenth and sixteenth centuries—a persecution that was fundamental to defining women's social position within the capitalist regime. It was to better understand the relationship between the witch hunt and the development of capitalism that I continued my research on the period of transition from feudalism to capitalism, starting from medieval social movements, which resulted in a new book: *Caliban and the Witch: Women, The Body and Primitive Accumulation,* published in 2004.[6]

In the 1990s, I also began to work a good deal on the question of education, partly in connection with my experience in Nigeria (having witnessed the World Bank's assault on public education in Africa), and partly because a cultural battle was taking place in the scholarly arena in the United States at the time: conservative intellectuals and professors had launched a crusade against all books and essays criticizing the canons of "Western civilization." In 1995, I edited an anthology titled *Enduring Western Civilization: The Construction of the Concept of Western Civilization and Its "Others."*[7] My goal with this book was to show that there is no such thing as Western civilization, that this concept is a fiction, a fabrication of Cold War ideology.

My work in this field, however, has been the struggle against the globalization and commercialization of education. It was oriented mainly toward denouncing the dismantling of education in Africa and mobilizing organizational support by North American teachers and students to get involved in the struggle of African teachers and students against structural adjustment. In this regard, some colleagues, mainly from Africa, and I founded an organization called the Committee for Academic Freedom in Africa (CAFA), in which academic freedom was interpreted as being the right to education. CAFA was formed in response to the attack conducted, in the name of "structural adjustment," against the education systems in Africa and in other "third world" countries in the 1980s and 1990s. Since then, we have seen the same type of development in Europe, and also in the United States, where the commercialization and corporatization of education is ongoing.

For thirteen years, I was one of the co-editors of the newsletter published by CAFA, which documented the struggles of students and teachers in Africa against budget cuts to education and the dismantlement of public education systems in most African countries. In 2003, three years after publication of *A Thousand Flowers: Social Struggles against Structural Adjustment in African Universities,* which I co-edited, CAFA and its newsletter ceased activity.[8]

Even though the CAFA newsletter wasn't widely distributed, it played a very important role, as CAFA was the only organization of this type outside Africa, and the newsletter was the only publication during those years that documented the growth of a pan-African student movement. Some of the documents published in the newsletter were reprinted in *A Thousand Flowers*.

For seven years, from 1995 to 2002, I was also engaged in a campaign against the death penalty. In 1995, some other radical philosophers and I formed the Radical Philosophy Association's Anti-Death Penalty Project, the goal of which was to mobilize students and professors in this cause. Mainly, I was trying to develop a feminist perspective on the death penalty, to convince feminists to become engaged in this struggle.

Here again, as it was for the question of war, there were two opposed feminist positions. The first, the liberal position, saw the state as the saviour-protector of women and supported cooperation between women and the police to make the neighbourhood "safer." The other position refused to treat social problems as criminal problems. It took into consideration the true sources of crimes and questioned the biased and unilateral way in which crime is defined in this society: for example, work-related accidents and deaths due to environmental contamination were never considered to be criminal acts.

LT: Do you think that Wages for Housework analyses are still relevant today? And how could they be updated?

SF: Yes, I think they're still relevant, for a number of reasons. To start with, it is clear that the first task to undertake in the struggle is to adopt programs that can bring people together, that can unite them and undermine the hierarchies built on the division of labour. This is where the strategic importance of the Wages for Housework strategy lay—and still lies—because domestic work, reproductive work, is a question that affects all women and can therefore constitute a field of political reunification among us.

Second, the Wages for Housework perspective is still relevant because the capitalist reorganization of labour that occurred in the 1980s and 1990s (Reaganism, Thatcherism, neoliberalism, globalization) resulted in a direct attack on public resources devoted to reproduction (health, education, working conditions, and so on), an attack on the means of reproduction, which produced a very large crisis in reproduction.

Third, the sphere of unpaid work, instead of shrinking, has considerably expanded in the last two decades. In effect, we have seen the reappearance of slave-like labour conditions, even in industrialized countries, with the proliferation of sweatshops, the change from welfare to workfare, the development in the United States of a mass incarceration regime within which prison labour is often appropriated, overexploitation and criminalization of undocumented immigrants, and deployment in the "third world" of food-for-wages programs.[9] More than ever, unpaid work and devaluation of labour power—which is the devaluation of our actual lives—are essential components of capitalist development. The Wages for Housework politics is therefore still current.

Today, however, the Wages for Housework perspective and struggle need a broader basis. It is not enough to demand just a paycheque; we must also demand other means of reproduction less subject to monetary manipulations: houses, health services, communal spaces, urban collective food-producing gardens where people may sow and harvest.

Everywhere, the struggle over reproduction is very openly also a struggle for reappropriation of the land, and also for the control of territory. All dimensions of the land question are fundamental. Earth, water, air, the ocean, as well as health and education, must be considered common goods, not subject to market logic.

LT: What do you think of the evolution of feminism today?

SF: There is not a single feminism; there are feminisms. With the intervention of the United Nations in feminist politics, we have seen an attempt to institutionalize the movement in order to defuse and neutralize its struggles and its subversive potential. We have also seen an attempt to redefine the feminist program to make it compatible with the neoliberal program. Since 1975, starting with the UN conference on women in Mexico City, the United Nations has tried to delegitimize all feminism that is not compatible with the needs of international capital, in the same way as it tried to dominate the anticolonial movement in the 1960s by ensuring that decolonization was compatible with the needs of ex-colonial powers and the United States.

With its global conferences on women, the United Nations has created "global feminism," with a category of feminists who believe that they have the right to define what women want, what the feminist program is, what a legitimate claim is and isn't.

At the same time, feminism has become internationalized. Its battlefield has shifted to the international stage. And today there exists a feminist movement, what in Latin America is called "popular feminism," that formed in response to liberalization of the world economy and has grown up outside of the institutional constraints of the United Nations, creating forms of reproduction outside of the market and the state. For me, that is real feminism. I think, for example, of women's movements in Chile, Argentina, and Peru, which, in the 1980s and 1990s, built forms of reproduction oriented toward self-subsistence and organized collectively.

However, institutional feminism has caused great damage, in my view, because it has neutralized the subversive potential of the feminist movement and created a state feminism that has served to confuse and disarm many women. For "global feminism," the problems are no longer, or not mainly, the policies that emerge from the global development of capitalism and their effects on women, but the fact that women pay a disproportionate price compared with men, because of the restructuring of the global economy.

LT: Can you expand on this last point?

SF: I mean to say that for "global feminism" (the feminists who follow the political program of the United Nations), the problem is not the capitalist development and recolonization that flow from the restructuring of the global economy. Rather, the problem resides in the fact that the policies of the International Monetary Fund and the World Bank have imposed an "unequal burden" on women. It is presumed that if women and men were to suffer equally, the structural adjustment and globalization of the economy would be more acceptable. The main concerns covered by these policies are gender relations, considered mainly in the context of the family but outside of capitalist relations. I explained this in greater detail in an essay published in *Revolution at Point Zero*.[10]

LT: Has Western feminism played a role in this evolution or this political appropriation?

SF: Certainly. The European and American feminist movements have played a large role in it. But we should not speak of "Western" feminism as if it were something uniform and monolithic. It must be noted that when we talk about Western feminism, we are talking about liberal feminism, which is highly visible because it is the only feminism that the media and the institutional political system recognize. Because of the activity of liberal feminism, which is integrated into United Nations policy, all anticapitalist struggles are now excluded from the official women's movement.

Global feminism boils down to a question of rights and a struggle for wage parity and equal working conditions. But we have been able to observe that integration into the organization of waged labour cannot constitute a factor in economic and political emancipation, even if it is an economic necessity.

As we have seen, the entry en masse of women into waged workplaces has given them more autonomy with regard to men but has changed working conditions little. For example, in most workplaces, there is no daycare. There is no reduction in work hours; on the contrary. It is recognized today that waged workplaces are still organized as if everyone who worked there had a woman at home. In the United States, there is no maternity leave; such leaves must be negotiated on an individual basis with each employer. This means that women must forget their gender to have waged work.

LT: What do you think of the struggle to include women's unpaid work in countries' national (satellite) accounts?

SF: It's a legitimate struggle, but with a very limited range. I am suspicious of the fact that the work would be "counted" rather than "paid." The question becomes, what does it count for? For purely moral recognition? Or is it a compensatory gesture that leaves everything unchanged? I am particularly suspicious since the UN agencies, and the UN itself, adopted this recommendation in the Beijing Platform for Action.[11]

The UN has never been opposed to structural adjustment policies imposed in Africa, Latin America, and Asia by the World Bank and the International Monetary Fund, and it didn't bat an eye when public pension systems and other social programs were dismantled all over the world. So how is it possible that the UN might seriously envisage compensation for reproductive work?

I am tempted to make the following syllogism, however, based on historical and political evidence: if the UN supports such a recommendation, it's because it cannot have any serious meaning, for the UN is compromised in this new world order and with the liberalization/ globalization programs founded on the suppression of all forms of social welfare—which has ravaged the life of women throughout the planet.

LT: What should we think of the fact that history has forgotten the Wages for Housework strategy and the groups that carried on the struggle?

SF: The situation seems to have changed. Today, feminists—and social movements in general—are showing a good deal of interest in Wages for Housework, and especially in the question of reproduction. In all the conferences of various social movements in which I've participated recently, there were workshops on Wages for Housework and on reproduction. Young women and men who, a few years ago, were paying no attention to the question of wages, are now writing dissertations on the subject. It is also interesting to observe that the underlying Wages for Housework theory—that housework is work, the work of producing and reproducing labour power, a socially necessary work—this theory is now widely acknowledged in the academic world, and also by the left and by most feminists, as it has become "common sense." At the same time, however, its political implications are still ignored, except for the recommendation that housework should be counted, which is very meagre satisfaction, in my view.

However, it is true that starting in the late 1970s, and in the years that followed, Wages for Housework was almost forgotten by most feminists. In the United States, one of the consequences of this historical forgetfulness was the incapacity of the feminist movement to defend welfare women from the stigmatization to which they were increasingly subjected. They began to be presented as social parasites, and they were stripped of the gains resulting from the struggles that their mothers and they themselves had led in the 1960s within the Welfare Movement.[12]

If the feminist movement had struggled for a redefinition of housework and had placed it on the same level as other forms of work, it would have been less easy to stigmatize women on welfare (especially in the United States, where women receive allowances from the Aid for Dependent Children program) and to cut these programs.

The forgetting of the Wages for Housework political strategy is symptomatic of the oblivion into which the entire question of reproduction fell in the 1980s and 1990s in North America. Starting in the mid-1970s, most feminists in the United States abandoned reproduction as a field of struggle, concentrating all their efforts on the question of equality (the Equal Rights Amendment) and access to waged work. As a consequence, today, women in the United States don't benefit from a right that is recognized for women almost everywhere else—the right to a maternity allowance. As I said, in the United States, women must negotiate this in their workplaces. It is not a parental right recognized by the state.

This is another reason for the exhaustion of the radical potential of the women's movement. The fact that the women's movement abandoned reproduction as a field of struggle meant that it was not able to reproduce itself. Now, women work in two workplaces: in the home and outside the home. They don't have the time to mobilize. I think that is one of the reasons the feminist movement was not capable of surviving and opposing the crisis of the 1980s, when the rights of all workers and all our living conditions were attacked.

We see the result today: we have lost many social programs; we work harder than ever before and continue to do most of the housework (even if middle-class women have been able to "free" themselves from housework by hiring other women as maids). Childcare and healthcare remain inaccessible, except at exorbitant costs that are prohibitive for most women; we have even become the "poor of the nation" (if the concept *feminization of poverty* has meaning); we work so hard that we don't even have time for family relations—not to mention political activity. This scenario is quite different from the one for which many of us, in the women's liberation movement, struggled in the 1970s!

But this won't have been the first time that the feminist movement has gone underground, if I can put it that way, and then resurfaced. The problems are still there. It becomes clearer and clearer to all women that accessing a second job does not lead to liberation and that it is not a strategy for attaining this goal. Similarly, it is now obvious that having the right to vote also doesn't mean liberation, even though women struggled hard to obtain it in the early twentieth century.

As for forgetting the groups that led the Wages for Housework struggle, this situation, as I said, is changing. I should note that these groups were not the only ones to be marginalized. All feminist groups that defied the status quo suffered the same fate. I'm thinking, for example, of those that struggled against nuclear rearmament in the late 1970s.

All of these groups that challenged the established order were marginalized in part because of the absence of media coverage or because of media distortion in the coverage of them. In particular, they were neutralized politically, notably through the funding of liberal groups and their publications, and also through the development of academic feminism, which holds the appropriate discourse on the movement. One day, perhaps, we will be able to better understand what initiatives were deployed by governments to provoke the dismantling of feminist groups that question social hierarchies and inequalities.

But I want to end on a positive note: we are now seeing a change among the younger generations of women. This has been clearly demonstrated by the Occupy movement, in which women have played a central role.

LT: What have been your intellectual and activist concerns since 2000? We could start with your interest in the witch hunt, which gave rise to a book on the subject in 2004, *Caliban and the Witch,* now translated into several languages.

SF: After I came back from Nigeria, I returned to the work that I had started on the question of the witch hunt, situating it in the broader context of the phase of "primitive accumulation" of capitalism.[13] As I explained in the introduction to *Caliban and the Witch,* this new research was greatly influenced by my comprehension of the effects of the restructuring of the world economy that I could observe first-hand in Nigeria.

The feeling that we were witnessing a new phase of primitive accumulation accompanied me all throughout the writing of *Caliban and the Witch,* to the point that my reading of the past was always filtered through the experience of globalization. I think that is one of the reasons the book has been so successful and has been published in so many languages—Spanish, German, Greek, Turkish, and French. Now, it is in the process of being translated into Italian, Serbian, Slovenian, Polish, and Japanese. I really didn't expect it! But I am convinced that it is because it provides a historical analysis and a theoretical framework that also sheds light on the present and, more importantly, enables us to identify the deep forces and mechanisms that structure the expansion of capitalist development and are required by the expansion of capitalist relations.

When I began to work on this book, I had no idea that a new wave of witch hunts was unfolding in several parts of Africa and in India, Nepal, and Papua New

Guinea, clearly rooted in the changes activated by the process of economic liberalization.

Confronted with these new persecutions, I realized the significance of the work that I did on the transition from feudalism to capitalism. This work gave me a framework, enabling me to interpret these new witch hunts and see their continuity with the surge of violence against women that globalization has produced. More specifically, I could see, once again, that the witch hunting is directly related to the extinction of communal systems of land tenure and the attack against subsistence economies, starting with subsistence farming, which is done mostly by women and, for millions across the world, is a source of sustenance and autonomy.

However, it has become a target of international financial institutions—like the World Bank, which promotes the idea that agricultural relations should be commercialized and that only money is truly productive of wealth. I have written several articles on the subject, including "Witch-Hunting, Globalisation, and Feminist Solidarity in Africa Today."[14]

Documenting and analyzing these new persecutions and the attempts that are being made to destroy all subsistence forms of production, for example through the promotion of microcredit, has been one of my main concerns in recent years. My work has gone in several directions. On one side, I've continued my analysis of the restructuring of the global economy and, in particular, the restructuring of the reproduction of labour power within it, its impact on the conditions of women, and women's resistance to it. My new book, *Revolution at Point Zero,* collects several articles that I wrote on this subject.[15]

I have also been very interested in documenting the efforts that people, women above all, are making in many parts of the world to create communal forms of existence and communal forms of production, both as a form of survival in the devastation produced in their community by capitalist development and as a way of reconstructing the social fabric lacerated by economic displacements, political repression, and privatization. All over the world, women are in the forefront not only defending the last remaining commons but also creating new ones. This has not been only theoretical work. Since the 1990s, as part of the antiglobalization movement in which I have been involved, I have been working with a broad network of people who are exploring, practically as well as theoretically, what today is the "politics of the commons" and how we can contribute to it.

Presently I have formally retired from teaching, but I still teach in many ways through workshops I conduct on different subjects. I write. I have recently been doing a lot of travelling, doing book tours, and I am involved with an international network of women working in various ways around the question of social reproduction. My approach to it has broadened quite a bit since the time of Wages for Housework. However, I am still convinced that this perspective was a powerful strategy, and I have never reneged on my views on the subject.

Silvia Federici and Louise Toupin (Photo: J. Keable)

Notes

Interview with Mariarosa Dalla Costa

1. Interviews with Mariarosa Dalla Costa were conducted between 1996 and 1998 and completed in 2013. The initial interview has been abridged.

2. Yann Moulier, "Avertissement pour *Ouvriers et capital* de Mario Tronti," in *Ouvriers et capital*, ed. Mario Tronti (Paris: Christian Bourgois, 1977), 13n7. This book is a classic of Italian workerism and its author is one of the prominent thinkers of the current. His most recent book is *Nous, opéraïstes. Le "roman de formation" des années soixante en Italie* (Paris: Éditions de l'Éclat and Éditions d'en bas, 2013). See also Harry Cleaver, *Reading Capital Politically* (Austin: Texas University Press, 1979).

3. Nick Witheford, "Cicli e circuiti di lotta nel capitalismo high-tech (I)," *Vis a vis* 4 (1996): 61, 64.

4. For an introduction to the thought of C.L.R. James, born in Trinidad and an important anticolonial leader during the 1950s and 1960s, readers may consult a dossier prepared about him by *Radical America* (4, 4 [1970]), in which his writings are excerpted. See also Paul Buhle, ed., *C.L.R. James: His Life and Work* (London: Allison & Busby, 1986). On Raya Dunayevskaya, see her contribution to the women's question: *Women's Liberation and the Dialectics of Revolution: Reaching the Future* (1985; repr., Detroit: Wayne State University Press, 1996). *Socialisme ou Barbarie* was the name of a group and its eponymous journal that was published from March 1949 to 1965. The group's objectives and program are described

in Cornelius Castoriadis, *La société bureaucratique 2: La révolution contre la bureaucratie* (Paris: UGE, 10/18, 1973), 395–417, in the chapter titled "Conceptions et programme de Socialisme ou Barbarie."

5. *Comando capitalistico*, translated here as "capitalist command," is a fundamental concept of "autonomy" thought. The term appeared in Italy, among Marxist autonomists, to describe capitalist domination. It evokes the "commandment" itself, those who are "commanded" and who may resist, defy, and break this commandment. The term therefore involves not only the faculty of capital to command and dominate society but also, and above all, the means implemented by workers in their struggles to subvert and break the ability of capital to command society. I am grateful to Harry Cleaver, expert in "autonomy" thought, for having shared with me the general lines of this definition.

6. *Omphalos* is a Greek word that may be translated as "the navel of the world."

7. Workerism (*Operaismo*) was a critical current of Italian Communism of the 1960s. On the historical roots of this current, see Cleaver, *Reading Capital Politically* (Austin: University of Texas Press, 1979), 45–62. For a synthesis of the main notions of workerism, see Harry Cleaver, "Autonomist Marxism," syllabus for a course given at the University of Texas, utexas.edu. See also Massimo De Angelis, "Interview with Harry Cleaver," 1993, utexas.edu; published first in Italian, "*Intervista a Harry Cleaver a cura di Massimo De Angelis*," *Vis a vis: Quaderni per l'autonomia di classe* 1 (Autumn 1993): 79–100. Finally, see Mario Tronti, "Social Capital," *Telos* 17 (Fall 1973): 98–121.

8. See Louise Toupin, *Wages for Housework: A History of an International Feminist Movement, 1972–77,* trans. Käthe Roth (London / Vancouver: Pluto / University of British Columbia Press, 2018): 85–97.

9. Pia Turri, a primary-school teacher and Wages for Housework movement activist in Italy, was very active in these groups and wrote the first texts on the question of "prostitution" in the Wages for Housework perspective. See "*Le mogli di tutti*," in *Il Personale è politico: Quaderni di Lotta Femminista* 2 (Turin: Musolini, 1973): 51–62. She also made a major contribution on the question of the school in the Wages for Housework perspective. For an outline of her thought, see Toupin, *Wages for Housework*, 71–74.

10. This book, *Donne, sviluppo e lavoro di riproduzione*, was translated into English as *Women, Development and Labor of Reproduction: Struggles and Movements*, ed. Mariarosa Dalla Costa and Giovanna Franca Dalla Costa (Trenton, NJ: Africa World Press, 1997).

11. The colloquium was held at the University of Quebec at Montreal on November 16–17, 1984. The proceedings were published by éditions VLB in 1986 as *L'Italie, le philosophe et le gendarme*, edited by Marie-Blanche Tahon and André Corten. Her presentation was later published as "Domestic Labour and the Feminist Movement in Italy since the 1970s," *International Sociology* 3, 1 (March 1988): 23–34.

12. See Mariarosa Dalla Costa and Selma James, *Power of Women and the Subversion of the Community* (Bristol, UK: Falling Water Press, 1975), 52n16.

13. See Mariarosa Dalla Costa, "*Riproduzione e emigrazione*," in *L'operaio multinazionale in Europa*, ed. Alessandro Serafini (Milan: Feltrinelli, 1974). This article was translated into English: "Reproduction and Emigration," *The Commoner* 15 (Winter 2012): 95–157, commoner.org.

14. Dalla Costa and James, *Power of Women*, 25–26, emphasis in original.

15. Mariarosa Dalla Costa, "Capitalism and Reproduction," in *Open Marxism*, vol. 3: *Emancipating Marx*, eds. W. Bonefield, R. Gunn, J. Holloway, and K. Psycopedis (London: Pluto Press,

1995), 1–16, reprinted at commoner.org, *The Commoner* 8 (2004); Mariarosa Dalla Costa, *"L'indigeno che è in noi, la terra cui apparteniamo," Vis a vis* 5 (1997): 73–100, translated into English: "The Native in Us, the Land We Belong To," *Common Sense* 23 (1998), reprinted at commoner.org.uk, *The Commoner* 6 (2003); Mariarosa Dalla Costa, *"Neoliberismo, terra e questione alimentare," Ecologia politica* 1 (1997): 84–91, translated into English: "Some Notes on Neoliberalism, on Land and on the Food Question," *Canadian Woman Studies / Les cahiers de la femme* 17, 2 (Spring 1997): 28–31, also in *Women in a Globalizing World: Transforming Equality, Development, Diversity and Peace*, ed. Angela Miles (Toronto: Inanna Publication and Education, 2013), 189–94; *Donne e politiche del debito*, translated into English as Mariarosa Dalla Costa and Giovanna F. Dalla Costa, eds., *Paying the Price: Women and the Politics of International Economic Strategy* (London: Zed Books, 1995); *Donne, sviluppo e lavoro di riproduzione*, translated into English as Mariarosa Dalla Costa and Giovanna F. Dalla Costa, eds., *Women, Development and Labor of Reproduction: Struggles and Movements* (Trenton, NJ: Africa World Press, 1999).

16.   Giovanna Franca Dalla Costa, *Un lavoro d'amore. La violenza fisica componente essenziale del "trattamento" maschile nei confronti delle donne* (Rome: edizioni delle donne, 1978), translated into Japanese in 1991 and into English in 2008: *The Work of Love: Unpaid Housework, Poverty and Sexual Violence at the Dawn of the 21st Century*, trans. Enda Brophy (Brooklyn: Autonomedia, 2008). For a summary, see Chapter 2 of Toupin, *Wages for Housework*.

17.   These materials were collected by Mariarosa Dalla Costa, who recently donated them to the Municipal Library of Padua. They are found in the following archive collections: Archivio di Lotta Femminista per il Salario al Lavoro Domestico, Donazione Mariarosa Dalla Costa (Archives de Lotta Femminista pour le

salaire au travail domestique, Gift of Mariarosa Dalla Costa).
Address: Biblioteca Civica, Centro Culturale Altinate/San
Gaetano, Via Altinate 71, 35121 Padova. Tel.: 0498204811. Fax:
049 820 4804. Email: biblioteca.civica@comune.padova.it.
padovanet.it.

18.   For instance, Leopoldina Fortunati, *L'arcano delle riproduzione:
Casalinghe, prostitute, operai e capitale* (Venice: Marsilio,
1981), translated into English: *The Arcane of Reproduction:
Housework, Prostitution, Labor and Capital*, trans. Hilary
Creek (Brooklyn: Autonomedia, 1995). See also Silvia Federici
and Leopoldina Fortunati, *Il Grande Calibano: Storia del
corpo sociale ribelle nelle prima fase del capitale* (Milan:
FrancoAngeli, 1984); Mariarosa Dalla Costa, *Famiglia, welfare e
stato tra Progressismo e New Deal* (Milan: FrancoAngeli, 1983),
English translation: *Family, Welfare, and the State: Between
Progressivism and the New Deal*, trans. Rafaella Capanna
(New York: Common Notions, 2015).

19.   See English translation: Mariarosa Dalla Costa, "Development
and Reproduction," in Dalla Costa and Dalla Costa, *Women,
Development and Labour of Reproduction*, reprinted at
thecommoner.org, *The Commoner* 10 (2005). See also Dalla
Costa, "Capitalism and Reproduction."

20.   Following the assassination of Italian politician Aldo Moro in
1978 by the Red Brigades, Italy went through an unpreced-
ented wave of repression, such that any activist activity was
very strongly impeded for several years.

21.   Dalla Costa, *Famiglia, welfare e stato*. See also Mariarosa Dalla
Costa, "Famiglia e welfare nel Dew Deal," *Economia e lavoro* 19,
3 (July–September 1985): 149–52, English translation: "Family
and Welfare in the New Deal," in *Women and the Subversion
of the Community: A Mariarosa Dalla Costa Reader* (Oakland,
CA: PM Press, 2019).

22.   See, notably, Mariarosa Dalla Costa, "Percorsi femminili e
politica della riproduzione delle forza-lavora negli anni '70,"

La Critica sociologica 61 (1982): 50–73; "Politiche del lavoro e livelli di reddito: E le donne?" *Sociologia del lavoro* 26–27 (1985–86): 155–70; "Fuori dal mulinello," in AAVV, *Crisi delle politiche e politiche nella crisi* (Naples, Libreria L'Ateneo, 1981), 93–104; "La femme entre la famille et les politiques de l'emploi en Italie," in *Les rapports sociaux de sexe: Problématiques, méthodologies, champs d'analyses. Actes de la table ronde internationale des 4–5 et 6 novembre 1987, Cahiers de l'APRE* [Paris], 7 (April–May 1988): 121–27.

23.   Mariarosa Dalla Costa, "Domestic Labour in the Feminist Movement in Italy since the 1970s," *International Sociology* 3, 1 (March 1988): 23–34; "Emergenza femminista negli anni '70 e percorsi di rifiuto sottesi," in *La società italiana, crisi di un sistema*, ed. G. Guizzardi and S. Sterpi (Milan: FrancoAngeli, 1981): 363–75; "Percorsi femminili."

24.   The term "double presence" used by Italian academics (*doppia presenza*) corresponds roughly to the notion of family-job reconciliation. For a critique of this notion, see Louise Toupin, "Le féminisme et la question des 'mères travailleuses': Retour sur le tournant des années 1970," *Lien social et Politiques* 36 (Autumn 1996): 69–75.

25.   See Mariarosa Dalla Costa, "Emigrazione, immigrazione e composizione di classe in Italia negli anni '70," *Economia e lavoro* 4 (October–December 1981). This article was the complement to a previous article on, among other things, emigration: Mariarosa Dalla Costa, "Riproduzione e emigrazione," published in English in *The Commoner* 15 (2012), commoner.org.

26.   Elisabeth Burgos, *I, Rigoberta Menchú: An Indian Woman in Guatemala*, ed. and intro. Elisabeth Burgos-Debray (New York: Verso, 1984); Vandana Shiva, *Staying Alive: Women, Ecology and Development* (London: Zed Books, 1989); Vandana Shiva and Maria Mies, *Ecofeminism* (London: Zed Books, 1993).

27.   The organizations were Via Campesina and the Community

Food Security Coalition. For other examples, see Dalla Costa, "L'indigeno che è in noi."

28. See, for example, Dalla Costa, "Capitalism and Reproduction"; "Development and Reproduction"; "Some Notes on Neoliberalism"; "L'indigeno che è in noi"; Dalla Costa and Dalla Costa, *Paying the Price*.

29. Marcos talked expressly about menstruation in his book *Yo Marcos* (Mexico City: Editiones del Milenio, 1996).

30. For a definition of primitive accumulation, see "Interview with Silvia Federici" below, note 2.

31. Mariarosa Dalla Costa, "*L'isterectomia: Un punto di vista di donna su risvolti storici e quesiti etici*," presentation given to the congress organized by the Società Italiana di Ginecologia e Ostetricia in Palermo, December 7, 1997. See also Mariarosa Dalla Costa, ed., *Isterectomia: Il problema sociale di un abuso contro le donne*, 3rd ed. (1998; repr., Milan: FrancoAngeli, 2002), translated into English: *Gynocide, Capitalist Patriarchy and the Medical Abuse of Women* (Brooklyn: Autonomedia, 2007).

32. "Personal injury," according to the Italian penal code at section 582 c.p. and "very serious" at section 583, paragraph 2, point 3.

33. Mariarosa Dalla Costa and Dario De Bortoli, "*Per un'altra agricoltura e un'altra alimentazione in Italia*," *Foedus* 11 (2005), English translation: "For Another Agriculture and Another Food Policy in Italy," *The Commoner* 10 (Spring–Summer 2005), commoner.org.

34. Articles written by Mariarosa Dalla Costa on these themes were published in a Spanish-language book, *Dinero perlas y flores en la reproduccion feminista* (Madrid: Akal, 2009). Some of these articles are available in an English translation in the online magazine *The Commoner*: "The Native in Us, the Land We Belong To," 6 (2002); "Capitalism and Reproduction," 8 (2005); "Development and Reproduction," 10 (2003); "Seven Good Reasons to Say Locality," 6 (2002);

"Reruralize the World," 12 (2007); "Two Baskets for Change," 12 (2007); "Food as Common and Community," 12 (2007); "Food Sovereignty, Peasants, and Women," 13 (2008); "So That Fish May Flop in Vegetable Gardens," 15 (2012). "Rustic and Ethical" was published in *Ephemera: Theory and Politics in Organization* 7, 1 (April 2007), 107–16, ephemerajournal.org. See also Dalla Costa, "Some Notes on Neoliberalism."

35.   Mariarosa Dalla Costa, "La puerta del huerto y del jardin," *Noesis, Revista de Ciencias Sociales y Humanidades* (Universitad Autonoma de Ciudad Juarez) 15, 28 (July–December 2005): 79–100, English translation: "The Door to the Garden," in W*omen and the Subversion of the Community*.

36.   Mariarosa Dalla Costa and Monica Chilese, *Nostra madre Oceano: Questioni e lotte del movimento dei pescatori* (Rome: DeriveApprodi, 2005), English translation: *Our Mother Ocean, Enclosures, Commons and the Global Fishermen's Movement*, trans. Silvia Federici (New York: Common Notions, 2014).

37.   On the relationship with the ecosystem, see Mariarosa Dalla Costa, "Fishermen and Women for Food Sovereignty," *The Commoner* 13 (2008), commoner.org.

38.   Mariarosa Dalla Costa, "La sostenibilidad de la reproduccion: De la luchas por la renta a la salvaguardia de la vida," in *Laboratorio feminista: Transformaciones del trabajo desde una perspectiva feminista; Produccion, reproduccion, deseo, consumo* (Madrid: Terradenadie Ediciones, 2006).

Among the most recent articles by Mariarosa Dalla Costa on the situation of women are the following, published in the online magazine *The Commoner*: "To Whom Does the Body of This Woman Belong?" 13 (2009); "Women's Autonomy and Remuneration of Care Work in the New Emergencies," 13 (2009); "Workerism, Feminism and Some Efforts of the United Nations," 15 (Winter 2012), commoner.org.

39.   The archives have been available since May 2014. For information on accessing them, see note 17.

Interview with Silvia Federici

1.   This interview was started in 1996 and completed in 2013.

2.   For Marx, primitive accumulation refers to the origin of cap-
     ital and the formation of the proletariat in the initial phase of
     capitalism (sixteenth–seventeenth centuries). The formation
     of the proletariat took place through, among other things,
     expulsion of peasants from the land, violent appropriation
     of communal land and that reserved for community use,
     and its use for private and commercial purposes. Primitive
     accumulation thus refers notably to the expropriation of the
     populations that use these common spaces (the commons),
     to their being pushed into the cities, and to their consecutive
     proletarianization (the Enclosure movement in England in
     the sixteenth century). It corresponds to the transition from
     communal agriculture that had assured people the means of
     their reproduction to a system of private landownership, the
     precondition for the transition from feudalism to capitalism.

3.   Midnight Notes was a collective, with members from several
     countries, that emerged from the antinuclear movement of
     the late 1970s. For almost thirty years, Midnight Notes pro-
     duced an analysis of capitalist development that, like the
     Wages for Housework perspective, contested the centrality
     of waged work in the class struggle and capitalist accumula-
     tion (see note 2 above, this interview). See zerowork.org.

4.   This was the third UN conference on women; the first took
     place in Mexico City in 1975, the second, called "the mid-
     decade for women," in Copenhagen in 1980.

5.   Silvia Federici and Leopoldina Fortunati, *Il Grande Calibano:
     Storia del corpo sociale ribelle nella prima fase del capitale*
     (Milan: FrancoAngeli, 1984). Leopoldina Fortunati was an
     activist of the Padua Wages for Housework group. She had
     pursued research in the field of technology in the Wages for
     Housework perspective after publishing an important book
     in 1981 that was part of the intellectual heritage of the Wages

for Housework perspective: *L'arcano della riproduzione: Casalinghe, prostitute, operai e capitale* (Venice: Marsilio, 1981), translated into English as *The Arcane of Reproduction: Housework, Prostitution, Labor and Capital* (Brooklyn: Autonomedia, 1995). In my book, *Wages for Housework*, I did not analyze this book because it was published after the period covered by my study, which corresponded to the existence of the IFC (1972–77). For an overview of Fortunati's intellectual journey, see wikipedia.org.

6.   Silvia Federici, *Caliban and the Witch: Women, the Body and Primitive Accumulation* (Brooklyn: Autonomedia, 2004).

7.   Silvia Federici, ed., *Enduring Western Civilization: The Construction of the Concept of Western Civilization and Its "Others"* (Westport, CT: Praeger, 1995).

8.   Silvia Federici, George Caffentzis, and Oussiena Alidou, *A Thousand Flowers: Social Struggles against Structural Adjustment in African University* (Trenton, NJ: Africa World Press, 2000).

9.   This is a program managed by the United States Agency for International Development (USAID) and applied in many African and South American countries, consisting of paying workers' wages not with money, but with food.

10.   See Silvia Federici, "Reproduction and Feminist Struggle in the New International Division of Labor," in *Revolution at Point Zero: Housework, Reproduction, and Feminist Struggle* (Oakland, CA / Brooklyn: PM Press / Common Notions / Autonomedia, 2012), 65–75.

11.   This is the platform adopted by the UN conference on women held in Beijing in 1995.

12.   See Milwaukee County Welfare Rights Organization, *Welfare Mothers Speak Out* (New York: W.W. Norton, 1972).

13.   See note 2 above (this interview).

14. Silvia Federici, "Witch-Hunting, Globalisation, and Feminist Solidarity in Africa Today," *Journal of International Women's Studies* 10, 1 (2008): 21–35, bridgew.edu.

15. Federici, *Revolution at Point Zero*.

Silvia Federici is a feminist writer, teacher, and militant. In 1972 she was cofounder of the International Feminist Collective that launched the Wages for Housework campaign. Her books include *Witches, Witch-Hunting, and Women*; *Caliban and the Witch*; *Re-enchanting the World*; and *Revolution at Point Zero*.

Mariarosa Dalla Costa was born in Treviso, Italy, in 1943. She studied at the University of Padua, received her doctorate in law in 1967, and was a professor at the Istituto di Scienze Politiche e Sociali. She is the author of the founding document of the Wages for Housework perspective published in 1972, translated into English as *The Power of Women and the Subversion of the Community*. She lives in Padua, Italy.

Louise Toupin lives in Montreal, Quebec. She has taught political science at Université du Québec à Montréal. She was a member of the Quebec Women's Liberation Front (1969-71) and co-authored numerous anthologies of activist and feminist writings. She is the author of *Wages for Housework: A History of an International Feminist Movement, 1972-77*.

Käthe Roth was born in Montreal and now lives in Saint-Lazare, Quebec. She has been a literary translator and editor for more than twenty-five years. Her work includes over thirty translated books and essays of literary nonfiction on various subjects, including art, architecture, economics, history, and sociology, as well as fiction.

"The intellectual contributions of Silvia Federici and Mariarosa Dalla Costa were foundational to the development of social reproduction theory and the broader Marxist-Feminist tradition. But in these incredibly rich and wide-ranging conversations, we gain a fuller understanding of the lives, politics, and activism of these two seminal figures. *The Crisis of Social Reproduction* is a study in praxis."

Simon Black, professor, Department of Labour Studies, Brock University

"This book offers a fascinating look into the origins and evolution of the feminist thinking of two preeminent feminist activists. From their 1970s Wages for Housework action to their present day activism, the book offers an insightful analysis of the continued struggle to recognize women's labour and economic worth in the home, (paid) workplace, and the informal economy, in both the developing and developed world. Despite a history of both successes and defeats, the book offers a positive outlook for feminist activism."

Susana P. Miranda, author of *Cleaning Up: Portuguese Women's Fight for Labour Rights in Toronto*

"In *The Crisis of Social Reproduction* Toupin invites Federici and Dalla Costa to reflect on the Wages for Housework movement, its seminal texts and important lessons, and the relationship between political thinking, experience, and practice. As Federici says, we must 'learn to make a sustainable revolution.' Such a quest must be open to constant reconfiguration in order not to lose its sensitivity to social realities."

Nina Trige Andersen, historian, journalist, and activist